W9-BAQ-042

Natural DISASTERS
AN IMAGINATION LIBRARY SERIES

ASTEROID STRIKES

by Victor Gentle and Janet Perry

Gareth Stevens Publishing
A WORLD ALMANAC EDUCATION GROUP COMPANY

Please visit our web site at: www.garethstevens.com
For a free color catalog describing Gareth Stevens' list of high-quality books and
multimedia programs, call 1-800-542-2595 (USA) or 1-800-461-9120 (Canada).
Gareth Stevens Publishing's Fax: (414) 332-3567.

Library of Congress Cataloging-in-Publication Data

Gentle, Victor.
    Asteroid strikes / by Victor Gentle and Janet Perry.
        p. cm. — (Natural disasters: an imagination library series)
    Includes bibliographical references and index.
    ISBN 0-8368-2831-3 (lib. bdg.)
    1. Asteroids—Collisions with Earth—Juvenile literature. [1. Asteroids—
Collisions with Earth. 2. Disasters.] I. Perry, Janet, 1960- II. Title. III. Series.
    QB651.G46   2001
    523.44—dc21   00-051619

First published in 2001 by
Gareth Stevens Publishing
A World Almanac Education Group Company
330 West Olive Street, Suite 100
Milwaukee, WI 53212 USA

Text: Victor Gentle and Janet Perry
Page layout: Victor Gentle, Janet Perry, and Joel Bucaro
Cover design: Joel Bucaro
Series editors: Mary Dykstra, Katherine Meitner
Picture researcher: Diane Laska-Swanke

Photo credits: Cover, p. 15 Photofest; pp. 5, 21 NASA; p. 7 (top) © Science VU/Visuals Unlimited;
p. 7 (bottom) © Allen E. Morton/Visuals Unlimited; p. 9 © AP/Wide World Photos; p. 11 ©
P. Bierman/Visuals Unlimited; p. 13 © Roger Ressmeyer/CORBIS; p. 17 Reprinted with permission
of MIT Lincoln Laboratory, Lexington, Massachusetts; p. 19 Planetary Defense: Catastrophic Health
Insurance for Planet Earth, Fig. 3-4, 2025 and Spacecast 2020, at http://research.maxwell.af.mil,
United States Air Force, Air University, Maxwell AFB, AL

Printed in the United States of America

1 2 3 4 5 6 7 8 9 05 04 03 02 01

Front cover: *One of a series of small asteroids pummeling Earth
ahead of the "big one," this one heading for the Chrysler Building
in New York City — from the 1998 movie* Armageddon.

TABLE OF CONTENTS

Words that appear in the glossary are printed in **boldface** type the first time they occur in the text.

WIPE-OUT

About 65 million years ago, a large **asteroid** hit our planet near what is now the Yucatan Peninsula in Mexico. It plunged deeply into the Earth on impact — about 35 miles (56 kilometers). Billions of tons of rock were thrown into the sky and rained down for hours afterwards. Giant waves, called **tsunamis**, sped across the oceans and flooded coasts. Shock waves traveled through Earth's crust, triggering volcanic eruptions and more tsunamis on the other side of the planet. Dust, from the impact and the volcanoes, darkened much of the sky.

Most scientists today believe this asteroid caused the sudden **extinction** of many **species** of animals and plants, including the dinosaurs.

This is how artist Donald E. Davis pictures a giant asteroid hitting our planet 65 million years ago. The effect probably wiped out the dinosaurs and many other life forms on Earth.

IMPACTS A-PLENTY

Asteroids are small rocky planets. In our solar system, they range from the size of a baseball to about 580 miles (930 km) in **diameter** — one quarter the diameter of Earth's Moon. **Comets** are large chunks of ice and rock. **Meteoroids** are pieces of rocks in space, from dust-sized particles to the size of small asteroids.

Look at the Moon on a clear night. It is pitted with craters caused by comets, meteoroids, and asteroids. The Moon has no atmosphere to protect it. Earth's atmosphere, which is about 435 miles (700 km) thick, burns up most of the smaller space rocks that rain down on us. However, larger objects do get through. There are craters from large space rocks all over our planet.

Top picture: *All those dents are craters in the Moon's surface. This is what the land surface of Earth might look like if it had no atmosphere.*

Bottom picture: *Meteor Crater in Arizona is one of the best-preserved craters on Earth. It is about 0.75 mile (1.3 km) wide and 800 feet (244 meters) deep.*

TUNGUSKA!

In 1908, a large comet smacked into Tunguska, Siberia. The impact flattened trees in an area of over 1,000 square miles (2,590 square km). The trees were all scorched on the side facing the center of the blast. Scientists figure that the explosive force was about 1,000 times bigger than the atomic bombs dropped on Japan in World War II.

The comet struck Earth far away from the nearest city, and no deaths were reported. However, if that same fireball hit New York City today, it would probably destroy most of the buildings and kill millions of people.

An Australian scientist, Michael Paine, recently estimated that about 350 Tunguska-sized objects have hit the surface of our planet in the past 10,000 years.

Trees lie across the countryside near Tunguska in Siberia. This 1953 photograph was taken 45 years after a huge comet struck, leveling everything in sight.

Recent Impacts

Have there been any strikes from space objects in modern times — apart from the comet that hit Tunguska? Yes, plenty. However, we probably don't know about most of them. Here are a few that we do know about.

In 1490, an asteroid exploded high over China and rained rocks that killed 10,000 people. In 1886, an 880-pound (400-kilogram) stone plowed into an Arkansas field. A 60-ton **meteorite** was found in Africa in 1920. In 1984, a Japanese pilot saw an asteroid explosion that was 200 miles (320 km) wide in the upper atmosphere.

The world witnessed the impact of Comet Shoemaker-Levy 9 in 1994 as it hit the planet Jupiter, making a mess as big as Earth!

Tourists and local people admire the world's largest known meteorite. Named "Hoba West," the 60-ton meteorite was found in Namibia, a country in Africa.

PHEW! THAT WAS CLOSE!

In 1989, Asteroid 1989 FC buzzed Earth. It missed by only 430,000 miles (690,000 km). That may not seem close, but think about it. This large asteroid missed Earth by just six hours. It was about 1,150 feet (350 meters) wide, which is large enough to destroy the entire state of Texas.

In the 1990s, scientists discovered asteroids that they thought might hit Earth. Luckily, further study showed that they will miss our planet.

There are two asteroids that scientists *know* will come within 250,000 miles (400,000 km) of Earth — in the years 2004 and 2027. They will be close enough to hit our Moon. But there are many asteroids that scientists still *don't* know about.

Eugene Shoemaker, one of the astronomers who discovered the comet that hit Jupiter in 1994. Here he is using telescopic photography to search for near-Earth asteroids.

HOW REAL IS THE DANGER?

So what are the chances that a major asteroid will hit Earth during your lifetime? Will it be big enough to wipe out a small town, a large city, or all human life? Astronomer Michael Paine made these estimates in 1999 based on all he knew.

Size of asteroid	Chances of a hit in the next 50 years	What happens if this asteroid hits
33 feet (10 m) wide	100%: small asteroids of this size will hit our atmosphere a few times every year.	Each small asteroid will burn up in the atmosphere.
330 feet (100 m) wide	1 in 20 — or 5%: the same as a 100% chance of being hit once in the next 1,000 years.	It would make a crater about as big as Meteor Crater, Arizona, and would probably kill about a million people.
547 yards (500 m) wide	1 in 800: the same as a 100% chance of being hit one time in the next 40,000 years.	It could wipe out a country as big as Mexico, cause huge tsunamis, and kill about 35 million people.
0.62 mile (1 km) wide	1 in 2,000: the same as a 100% chance of being hit once in the next 100,000 years.	It would cause worldwide climate changes and kill about 63 million people.
6.2 miles (10 km) wide	1 in 2,000,000: the same as a 100% chance of being hit once in the next 100 million years.	This would be like the asteroid that killed the dinosaurs. We'd probably all be killed.

A large, glowing asteroid heads for a city in the United States — from the 1997 movie Asteroid. *In reality, a rock this size is more likely than a planet-killing monster asteroid.*

SEARCHING FOR ASTEROIDS

Some private groups and governments have begun to look for and track asteroids that might hit Earth. It's a big and expensive job. To do the job right, much more money and many more people are needed. One of the few big search efforts going on today is Spacewatch at the University of Arizona.

Scientists announced in June 2000 that about 900 "large" asteroids, 0.6 mile (1 km), or bigger may be a threat to Earth. Those asteroids are part of a huge system of rocks ranging from specks to 40 miles (64 km) wide. NASA's Near-Earth Asteroid Tracking System had identified 332 asteroids by January 2000. But most have not been spotted, and we don't know what course they are on.

This telescope at White Sands Missile Range, New Mexico, is used by the Lincoln Near Earth Asteroid Research (LINEAR) project to identify asteroids.

ASTEROID DEFENSE

What could we do about a "large" asteroid heading for us? That depends on how much time we'd have.

If we spotted a large asteroid today that wouldn't hit us for at least ten years, we'd have time to plan. We might send rockets armed with explosives to destroy the asteroid. More likely, we would use explosives to force the asteroid onto a different path.

If the asteroid was due to hit in five to ten years, then we'd probably have enough time to react. Scientists and governments around the world would have to work together to figure out how to handle the problem.

If the asteroid was due to hit us next year, we probably would not be able to stop it.

*Six ways we might protect Earth from an asteroid: a) put a rocket on it; b) shoot a bomb at it; c) push another asteroid into it; d) use high-powered **lasers** to blast it; e) use a **mass driver** to dig pieces out of the asteroid and shoot them into space; f) fix a **solar sail** to slow it down while Earth gets out of the way. — USAF Air University report, 1996.*

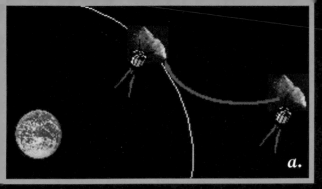

a.

b.

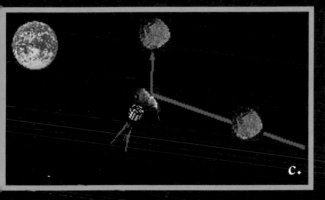

c.

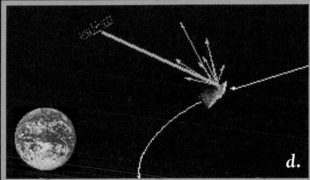

d.

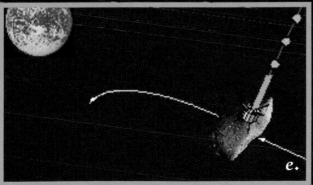

e.

f.

WE NEED TO DO MORE

It will take many years for NASA, Spacewatch, LINEAR, and other groups to identify just the "large" asteroids. What about all the others? Asteroids as small as 330 feet (100 m) could kill about a million people. There are tens of thousands of asteroids between this size and 0.62 mile (1 km) wide. Some of them are almost certainly on a course to hit Earth sooner or later.

Perhaps the nations of the world should try harder to find and track all the dangerous asteroids and comets. We are off to a good start by looking for the largest ones that could cause the greatest damage and most deaths.

But maybe that's not doing enough. What do *you* think?

An asteroid this big striking Earth might kill us all. The danger is real, even if the chance of being hit soon is small. Are we doing enough to avoid the fate of the dinosaurs?

More to Read and View

Books (Nonfiction)
Asteroid Impact. Doug Henderson (Dial)
Asteroids. Samantha Bonar (Franklin Watts)
Asteroids, Comets, and Meteors. Robin Kerrod (Lerner)
Cosmic Debris: The Asteroids. Isaac Asimov and Greg Walz-Chojnacki
   (Gareth Stevens)
Death from Space: What Killed the Dinosaurs? Isaac Asimov and
   Greg Walz-Chojnacki (Gareth Stevens)
Discovering Comets and Meteors. Isaac Asimov and Greg Walz-
   Chojnacki (Gareth Stevens)
If an Asteroid Hit the Earth. Ray Spangenburg and Kit Moser
   (Franklin Watts)
Powerful Waves. D. M. Souza (Carolrhoda)
The Ultimate Asteroid Book. Mary A. Barnes (Aladdin)

Videos (Nonfiction)
Asteroids: Deadly Impact. (National Geographic)
Cosmic Travelers — Comets and Asteroids. (Goldhil)
The Doomsday Asteroid. (WGBH/NOVA)

Videos (Fiction)
Armageddon. (Touchstone)
Asteroid. (Artisan)
Deep Impact. (Paramount)

WEB SITES

If you have your own computer and Internet access, great! If not, most libraries have Internet access. The Internet changes every day, and web sites come and go. We believe the sites we recommend here are likely to last and give the best and most appropriate links for our readers to pursue their interest in meteors, asteroids, tsunamis, plate tectonics, astroscience, and geoscience.

www.ajkids.com

Ask Jeeves Kids. This is a great research tool.
Some questions to try out in Ask Jeeves Kids:
Does the Moon's gravity affect meteors?
How do I find out if what I'm holding is a meteor or just another rock?

You can also just type in words and phrases with "?" at the end, for example:
Black Holes?
Satellites?
Stars?

janus.astro.umd.edu/astro/impact.html

Part of Astronomy Workshop, this interactive page allows you to select the size and make-up of a comet or asteroid hitting your favorite planet, and then to see the consequences.

www.ngdc.noaa.gov/seg/hazard/ hazards.shtml/

Natural Hazards Databases. In addition to an amazing photo gallery (click on slide sets) of earthquakes, tsunamis, volcanoes, and other natural hazards (and the debris they leave behind), there is a series of kids' quizzes on hazards ranging from volcanoes and earthquakes to wildfires and tsunamis.

whyfiles.org/106asteroid/

Asteroids on the attack! This section, from the University of Wisconsin's "Why Files" program, is a lively presentation of the issue of a real danger from space.

www.tsunami.org

Pacific Tsunami Museum. This is a cool site with many tsunami pictures. Whether a tsunami is caused by an undersea earthquake or an asteroid impact, it can be devastating to coastal areas.

www.EducationWorld.com/a_sites/ sites039.shtml

Watch some meteor showers at Education World.

www.discovery.com/stories/nature/ games/meteor.html

Launch a fireball at the Earth, see where it ends up, and quiz yourself on which historic meteor you've just pounded into Earth! Or, go to the home page of Discovery Kids at **kids.discovery.com/kids/home.html** and click on The List, go to number 36, and do the fun thing, here at Discovery.

GLOSSARY

You can find these words on the pages listed. Reading a word in a sentence helps you understand it even better.

asteroid (AS-ter-oyd) — a small planet or large rock from within our solar system 4, 6, 10, 12, 14, 16, 18, 20

comets (KAHM-ets) — huge balls of ice, rocks, and gases that travel through space, often trailing a glowing tail 6, 8, 14, 20

diameter (die-AM-eh-ter) — the width of a globe 6

extinction (ek-STINK-shun) — the end of life for an entire species 4

lasers (LAY-zerz) — narrow beams of intense light capable of carrying a lot of energy 18

mass driver — a machine like a large gun that uses electricity to make magnetic fields to shoot rocks or other things into space 18

meteorite (MEE-tee-or-ite) — rock or iron; part of an asteroid, comet, or meteoroid, after it has landed on Earth 10

meteoroid (MEE-tee-or-oyd) — a piece of rock traveling through space, as small as a speck of dust or as large as an asteroid 6

solar sail — a large sheet of material used in space to catch the "wind" of tiny specks that stream through space from the sun 18

species (SPEE-sheez) — members of a group of animals or plants that look like each other and can breed to make more of their kind 4

tsunamis (su-NAM-eez) — giant ocean waves caused by undersea earthquakes, undersea volcanoes, exploding bombs — or by impacts of asteroids, comets, or meteoroids 4, 14

INDEX